DOG STAR DELICATESSEN
New and Selected Poems
1979-2006

Other books by Mekeel McBride

The Deepest Part of the River
Wind of the White Dresses
Red Letter Days
The Going Under of the Evening Land
No Ordinary World

DOG STAR DELICATESSEN
New and Selected Poems
1979 - 2006

Mekeel McBride

Carnegie Mellon University Press

2006

ACKNOWLEDGMENTS

The author wishes to express her gratitude to the editors
of the following publications in which these poems first appeared:

Crying Sky:	I Begin Again Honey It Almost Seems Like Darkness
Four Corners:	Cabin in the Woods Like a Gospel Singer Swan-Winged in Hallelujahs
Georgia Review:	Apple Turning into Orchards

Lynx Eye:	Mirror
	Oracle, Brooch, Sunflower, Hors
	      d'oeuvre and Sailboat All
	      Packed Safely in the Good Old
	      Glowing Portmanteau

Porcupine:	Flower
Seneca Review:	Orchard
Virginia Quarterly Review:	Night Story: window
And heartfelt thanks, also, to:	Lysa James, Ronald Gehrmann, Charlotte Bacon, Julie Serrano, Larry Brickner-Wood, John Lofty, Jay Apt, Tory Poulin, Hanna Frank, Yuri Belopolsky, Dr. S. & Dusky

Book design by Christopher Boette

The publication of this book is supported by a grant from
the Pennsylvania Council on the Arts.

PENNSYLVANIA
COUNCIL
ON THE

ARTS

Library of Congress Control Number: 2005924492
ISBN- 13: 978-0-88748-424-7
ISBN- 10: 0-88748-424-7
ISBN- 13: 978-0-88748-434-6 Pbk.
ISBN- 10: 0-88748-434-4 Pbk.

10 9 8 7 6 5 4 3 2 1

CONTENTS

WIND OF THE WHITE DRESSES
1995

RED LETTER DAYS
1988

THE GOING UNDER OF THE EVENING LAND
1983

NO ORDINARY WORLD
1979

Flower

This flower is a sigh, a high-stakes gamble,
blind zap of power in the wire. Knows how
to time travel. No Zendo for this flower, no.
Says *Fuck you* and really means it.
This flower is pollinated by the dead.
Listens to the dial tone for hours.
Has been trained to seek spiritual advice
from the wind-chill factor. Though grateful,
could do with a little less bad weather.
Thinner than a dime, fatter than laughter.
This flower refuses to loiter inside
sleep's parking meter. Even rooted, can dance
like the devil. Aspires to be the corsage
on Dickinson's wrist as she weds the young Cornell
in a Galaxy Chapel. This flower is a holy terror.

DOG STAR DELICATESSEN

for Adeline Hoyle

The Dog Star, or Sirius—the "sparkling one"—is the brightest of the
fixed stars, over twenty times more luminous than the sun. It is part
of the constellation Canis Major, the greater dog, representing one of
Orion's hunting dogs.

Ancient Egyptians revered the Dog Star as the Nile Star or the Star
of Isis. Its yearly appearance at the summer solstice, June 21, signaled the
coming of the rising of the Nile, which sustained Egyptian agriculture.

The Dog Star is said to be fixed in place at the bridge of the Milky Way
where it keeps guard over the abyss as souls cross over to be reincar-
nated.

delicatessen n.pl. (< Fr. *delicat*) +*essen*, food (<*essen*, to eat); actually
< Fr. delicatesse, delicacy   1. prepared cooked meats, smoked fish,
cheeses, salads, relishes, etc. 2. a shop where such foods are sold.
                                            —*Webster's New World Dictionary*

Bella

He thinks he's going to build an addition
but finds rot in a wall, rips it out, finds more
in sills and floors and roof until finally
he's sledgehammered the house into rubble.
The whole house!

He seems so happy as he tells me this, the way
anyone else would be glad to find money
hidden in books or drawers or even
ice cube trays. It's late October and he's laughing.
Laughing! I ask where he's living.

In the garage, he says. Busy designing
the new house that will be open, wide
and full of light. I keep thinking
the weather's going to be bad soon,
how my lawn, a simple matter

compared to houses coming down, is always
the last to be mowed and raked. And what
would happen if I turned to find,
in the name of home repair, my house
in a heap on the leaf-strewn lawn?

Then I see the garage fall too, how I'd be
forced to live in ice, a gloom-igloo of my own
making, and before he can even get the next
sentence out, I've died, in my own mind at least,
from cold-induced dementia.

Wouldn't it be better to accept the rot, just paint
and paper to make the walls look solid and leave it
at that? Bella, his dog, who could not care less
about all this construction talk, shakes her head,
red leash in mouth. *If you won't walk me,*

I'll walk myself. If we're not going anywhere,
I'll dance in place. He tells me how Bella
keeps losing her tennis balls at the caved-in place
where the new house will take shape.
And then I know, this is the blessing only a dog

would be smart enough to offer: *Now's the time
let's play!* as she tosses from her soft mouth
the ball that means flying a stretch of open beach
over and over, amulet of pure happiness,
into the deepest part of the new foundation.

Oracle, Brooch, Sunflower, Hors d'oeuvre and Sailboat All Packed Safely in the Good Old Glowing Portmanteau

for Michael DePorte

And I turn and there's this moon, exactly
the one Chicky says you can't write about
anymore because it's been done, and it's old
and nobody cares. But it's my morning
and this full moon edges out of its sunrise nest
singing, *I am not the Hunter's moon*

because even something that far away knows
how sad I used to be with Abram Yosef Jack
who kept seven rifles under our bed, dead
and gutted deer hamstrung in the trees. And I
was one. I'm pretty sure this is something else
Chicky wouldn't like,

me saying the moon sang. But in its own way,
it did. And after *No longer Hunter's* I heard a pearl
turn into a word—whole—in parting
which made me so light-headed, I slipped
for awhile out of time to drift as it drifted
silently over the waking world like a great mother-

of-pearl platter, and it was leaving, all right, summer
shot to hell, too, with nothing to show for itself
but the trees falling to pieces. And a big sunflower
so burdened by the weight of its own life, its heavy head
lay flat against the earth, but in the end,
or so it seemed to me, only doubled over

in seed-heavy laughter. And Chicky can make
fun of the moon all he wants but he left a message,
once, on my machine, no words, just him, playing
the harmonica and if that music wasn't honeyed
with the kind of motion that lifts and fills
the white sail of the moon every night,

whether you can see it or not, then there is
no oxygen left on this earth but there's plenty,
of course, more than enough and that's the point,
isn't it, of a moon that floats like a glowing
suitcase down the night-into-sunrise river
of an ordinary October morning.

Heron

I listen with my body.
Tide takes and gives
and never stays
the same. My waiting's
made from patience
wide as the whole swath
of cloud-kissed river.
Heaven over, heaven
under. Invisible,
the little gods gather,
loving more
than anything the gift
of vista. And so
I still myself, my legs
especially, into reeds,
the slender trunks
of new trees. And when
the fish gentle themselves
into the cool shade
my meditation makes,
a flash of silver
breaks the mirror
and I take them easily,
each shining being,
into me. So once again,
the buried rise
on wise and patient
earthly wings.

The Well

The child falls into a well. Far away hole at the top
gives her a day that's round, all azure.

And at night, inky with a slight stain of a stars.
That little bit of glitter makes her think of seeds

she used to plant with her mother. The wonder
of sunflowers coming from something small and hard.

Sometime much later, a mouse brings her a petal.
It could have brought a golden kernel of corn,

a grain of rice. That part doesn't matter.
She presses the petal to her chest and sleeps,

a day, a decade, half a century. Who knows. Who really
ever knows. Sometimes, when she wakes, she is safe

at the edge of a soft green field. Sometimes, still deep
in the well, forgotten by everyone, even the mouse.

It Almost Seems Like Darkness

leaves her body last, as if, all along, that had been
the one thing keeping her alive. Now the air wavers,

grows cooler, like waking in sheets made of wind
that arrives just after rain, earth fragrant with longing

for what might restore it. But where is she now?
She was here. I thought I'd seen a dark green bridge,

like the one over Monet's water lilies. I thought
I'd been holding her hand. Outside the hospital window,

a sparrow settles on the concrete sill. It tilts its head
and turns to look again into the empty room.

Brown flower. Dust sister. I can't really see
its eye but know light's in it

from a place close by but growing distant.

Orchard

for John Lofty

He was your friend more than mine. The last time
I saw him, you stood together in late spring light
talking about his puppy. Then he unbuttoned
his oxford cloth professor's shirt, pleased to reveal
nova bursts of tie-dye—the exuberant
and wholly unexpected color of his undershirt

like one of those gorgeous photographs the Hubble
sends back of a new universe taking shape in a place
so far away it's almost impossible to imagine.
You thanked him for a fruit tree he'd given you
just now flowering with exceptional extravagance.
That's the last thing I heard him talking about—

a sky-drench of petals and good fruit soon.
Weeks later, a truck slams into his motorcycle
and he's gone. But last night, he came back,
sitting at a desk in an empty office, the kind you see
in old black and white movies where the private eye's
up all night. Only one light fixture overhead

and it's not moving an inch in this deep summer heat.
He's telling me about the poetry he writes
and never shows anyone, how those poems fill him
with private and delicious happiness. A secret
orchard, he says. I nearly forget what he's telling me
because I'm trying so hard to keep him here—

the way you freeze when a deer appears on the path
ahead of you—as if your breathlessness could stop
the wild thing from vanishing again
into seamless green. He stays with me until I wake.
Trying, I think, to get word to you,
who loved him so much that for a while

grief made of your dreams a drowned
and dreamless place. He wants you to know he is well
and finding his way. I saw it in his gentle eyes,
the way his hands rested so lightly, one
on top of the other, on the empty desk. No papers
left to grade. No watch strapped to his pale wrist.

Night Story: window

Last night, Jimmy was still alive. Thin as a kid in his soft green robe.
Everyone happy to help. I figured he'd made it onto the new medicine in
time. You were cooking a big pot of shrimp for friends and nurses. Our
friend Kishio had just drawn the Japanese characters for shrimp which
mean *old man* because of the creature's curved back. This time,
Jimmy wasn't going to die. It might still have been day but the sky was
old. You and I stood beside an open window washing curtains made
from the same fabric Mother Theresa's nuns wear. As we twisted out
rinse water, the blue and white cloth disintegrated, worn thin from such
a long love affair with light. In your plant-filled rooms, I was happier
than I had been in a long time, looking through all those unadorned,
open windows. . . .

Red Thread

It's just that there isn't
anything else left.
She cracks

an egg. Sun rises.
In the next room,
her mother is dying.

As she has done
these last few days,
the daughter ties red thread

to the foot
of her mother's bed
then trails the spool

out to the neglected
garden, looping
the last of it

to a tumble and storm
of roses that, despite
all the sorrow of the world,

cannot keep themselves
from slipping, rain-shocked,
into wild blossom.

Cabin on the Mountain

After you died, in the time when there was no
light left, no dream at all, I built it,
piece by piece, one wildflower
at a time on a lupine-blue mountain
that no real map can name.

I started with splinters because that is all
I had and found, after a while,
I had amassed a log. It was very slow work
and sometimes I got it all backwards
because of how sad I was:

the wood smoke drifting
its gray scarves skyward even before
I worked in the fire; the meandering creek
running right through where the bedroom
later rose. But it didn't matter

because slow and green as moss
a little peace from that dreamed-of place
began to stick to me. Not faith, not hope,
not even light. Just a sense, somewhere faraway,
of something all right.

And so I kept building—scraps
of sun-splashed meadow, a coyote
at the edge of things, curious
about the going's on but never quite
visible. And after a long time, it came together.

Just when that was I couldn't say.
It happened, that's all, the unexpected wholeness
of things, though now with some dark places
my dreaming can't do a thing about.
But I have come to accept that, too.

I Begin Again

Even though it was nearly three A.M., I was so lonely that when I heard the knock I opened the door. And there was someone who looked a lot like me. Except that when I said *So long*, she said *It's time*. And when I said *Too late* she walked right in. I tried to fool her with *I am the last* but she shot back *I begin again* and set to work arranging on the counter a row of tiny keys as shiny as new dimes and caught my tears in a cleaning rag then twisted it all into a tin cup and said *Drink* and I did, tasting stars.

Your Silence Made of Orchards

for Adam Vital
who owns the bass, though he does not
know how to play it

Bass who is elder sister to the cello,
instrument exactly the size
of a human, it is to you
I pledge my deepest allegiance.

Played or not, you are the earth
in which a man grows food
that will sustain him through hours
even the clock is afraid to name.

You are the tree truly rooted long after
the ax has had its way. Inside you,
light from the small fire of a lost explorer
burns on through the night.

This is about the low note that holds
everything together. There is such a note.
It keeps passing through you.
The last note and after that.

Your spirit, a seaside town early spring
before visitors return, waves leaving
at the edge of the dry world the most delicate
nightgowns of sea spray and tears.

Each morning how hopeful I feel
to find you, your silence made of orchards.
Music, all of it, surviving inside,
whether you are ever touched again or not.

Mirror

A pilgrim stops halfway across the bridge
to watch a padlocked chest drift down the river.
Whether it belongs to him or not
does not matter. What he needs, he carries
with him. It is not much. Soon he will be able
to set down even that small burden.

The room she kneels in is filled with light.
Dry grasses outside the window, tall and still.
One of her onyx hair combs has fallen,
black petal, onto the hardwood floor.
It is not her face she searches for as she gazes
into the shining water of the hand-held mirror.

The Bowl of Milk

for Yuri Belopolsky who told me
& for Metropolitan Anthony of Sourozh who told him

In the story, every night the shepherd
leaves a bowl of milk on the stone as a gift for God.
And in the morning, always, the bowl is empty.

Knowing how much God must love that milk,
the shepherd, too, is happy. Then a holy man
happens by and says, *You idiot. God has no*

appetite for this offering. God has no mouth,
no body. Who knows what happens to the milk.
Maybe animals drink it. Maybe your drunken brother.

But certainly not God. Later, in a sadness
made from deep hunger, the holy man says to God,
Can you believe this fool and his bowl?

But who is it, really, listening to this doubt so full
of secret longing? In the depths of the forest
there are wild thorny bushes where blackberries

sweeter than the heart of Jesus grow all summer
eaten only by birds. And when the answer comes
there are more who hear than you might think.

In that milk, a field of wildflowers rises
out of Auschwitz rubble. A child once chained
in an earthen cellar, hair shorn, now walks safely

through darkness, night-sheen sweet
on the long, loose wing of her unbound hair.
A doctor makes, of his own hand,

a soft bracelet around the wrist of the patient
to take a pulse, to give the reverent medicine
of gentle touch. In a body something like sunlight

on water, though infinitely finer, the dog
who has been dead now for years,
still walks in radiant patience beside the man

who so loved him. It is this the shepherd's milk
is made from and it is my prayer nightly answered
to bow and then drink deeply.

Honey

for Janet Martin

Just one? the maitre'd asks, with undue emphasis
on *just*. I say *Yes* and by the time I'm seated,
feel exactly like zero's lesser sister.

I've got a book, I've always got something
to make it look like I'm busy, as if I have a friend,
even if it's only paper.

Before the waitress gets to my table, I've overheard
she works here double shifts. Wal-Mart, too,
stocking shelves. And cleaning office buildings.

She's in her early forties, hair dyed black, cut short.
When I ask her for a chicken burger, she looks at me
and says, *Honey, intuition's telling me*

I'd bring the order and your face would fall.
So I'm going with my gut and telling you the truth.
That chicken isn't real.

It's from some factory, all breaded up
with God knows what. You look like the type
who wants things to be what they really are.

So for a dollar fifty more, you can get a sautéed breast,
with mayo, lettuce, fresh tomato. Now she's laughing,
a life-is-good laugh and anyone can tell that's real,

even though she's overworked, her face,
creased from years of chain-smoking and I'd guess,
bad boyfriends. Leans down, and whispers

Whatever it is, I've decided I have to let it out.
Her laughter's like dice full of good luck willing
to include anyone who wants in on the secret.

What happens next makes me happy to be
who I am and sitting at this table.
I see her take an old framed photo of this town—

trees, church and lawn—turn it upside down
and hang it that way so the steeple points
like a compass needle toward all of us together.

And the ground we'd thought was under us
becomes a kind of unexpected heaven. She smiles
at me, then whispers *Now let's see if anyone will notice. . .*

Like a Gospel Singer
Swan-Winged in Hallelujahs

Road construction detours me
along a small lake.
I'm late for work,
not even taking the time
to look for turtles sunning in sand

when a swan hits the water hard,
her wings raised
like a Gospel singer caught
trance-note-high in Hallelujahs,
breast breaking the calm surface

so that the pond seems to swell
up around her
in a crazy green crown
all jeweled with water lilies
and minnows.

It's an arrival that probably
happens every day although
I've never noticed
and makes me think of the musician
enduring hours of boredom

until the conductor's baton
finally points to her.
And she lets the bass drum have it—
a huge boom that's the Taj Mahal,
an enormous love palace,

blooming out of felt-headed stick
to drum skin, swan body
to lake. It rinses habit
right out of my day so that later,
when you catch my eye, something

that had been plain and close
to unnoticed, becomes
something else altogether
as the calm water breaks again
and the glad body enters.

Lucky

I'm late, need to pay, but he's ahead of me,
ordering ice cream for his dog. No chocolate.
The waitress suggests vanilla with just a tiny bit of fudge.
No chocolate, he says again. The exchange goes on like this
for a long time. Finally they settle on strawberry.

Now he wants a coffee, one sugar, no milk so he'll have
something to drink while the dog's eating. The bill
comes to three dollars. He empties a pocket,
gliding quarter after quarter across the counter,
savoring the slow slide of each cool coin.

By now, I'm so late there's no chance I'll get to where
I thought I was supposed to be so I give up and ask
What kind of dog? He takes his time in turning
to answer, *Pit bull*. A leashless pause.
And part Borzoi. A rescue. Her first trip downtown.

I wanted to get her something special so she'd know
it's safe among strangers. He's in his sixties
and handsome in the way that distant mountains
seem both beautiful and private. Now, late
is starting to feel like right on time. Grateful, I stop

outside to watch him drink, with such pleasure,
hot coffee in ninety degree weather. Gently,
he leans over to steady the paper cup of ice cream
for his dog, Lucky. Her tail's tucked between her legs
and I see in the way she looks up

that in her life before this there was never
the smallest pleasure without punishment.
She's afraid anyone, even the man holding the cup,
might start kicking her again. Except it all
tastes so rich and sweet and cool that she can't help

but give herself to the goodness of it with the almost
unbearable joy the abandoned feel when someone
kind finally turns to them, sees them,
really sees them and says, *You. It's you*
I have been waiting for all this time.

Midwinter Gift

Peace from the sleep
of hibernating animals
rises into the snowy field.
A pine alive with wind
holds the green torch
of itself steady as the world
goes to shadow. Beautiful
just as it is, this soft mend
of new snow over river,
spirit, meadow, road;
simple vista of the parts
quietly becoming whole.

Turtle

for Kerry Reilly

Even in a darkness this complete, you
can still see. The waves seem to reveal stars,
as if billions of them had been held captive
for centuries in the ocean's vaulted convent.
And now, the stunning topple of water
at the world's edge releases them into a night
that is just born and strangely safe
like breathing as you dance, like sleeping
in the highest branches of a tree that has survived
lightning and flood, blight and drought.

Other times, though, I know, there are
dark places that assemble in your spirit so that
it becomes impossible to see. No tide, no stars,
no start or end to anything, just endless drowning
but no dying. Even then, under the cold sand
you stand stranded on, turtle eggs are hatching,
little armored amphibians cracking out
of their moony white jails and moving jauntily
toward the sea with an ease that is both
happy-go-lucky stagger and star-sharp instinct.

How I'd love to press all of this into one word
so you could say it over and over, a word like *evening*
or *egg* or *aurora*, to help you remember when things
get hard, those turtles now waking alone in the dark,
then making their crazy dash for the dazzle and crash
of open ocean. The word I'd give you would mean
Don't care too much and *Care too much*. It would mean,

Look how easily that sweet wave's sweeping
toward shore folding into itself and taking home
pebbles and driftwood and sea glass and turtle.

Apple Fattening Into Orchards

At first, this tiredness seems simple like letters
children added or forgot altogether in words
they tried to spell—each child dropped, diamond
by sad diamond, from the tiara of chairs
for the finals of a spelling bee years ago.

A paper cup of coffee in this café does little to relieve
the sense of something missing. I'd be happiest
simply slipping out of my chair onto the floor
where in no time at all I'd be as zippered into sleep
as a base camp climber resting after Everest.

But what would that mechanic, showing his buddy
a new blue Corvette in *Autosport*, make of me
lying there like a crash test dummy broadsided
by exhaustion? Maybe nothing, and it's the slim string
of his disinterest that helps to keep me seated.

By now I'm as heavy as the mail sack a postal worker
buries, for reasons never disclosed, in his cellar.
And then it seems this tiredness is not so much
like misspelled words or letters that will never reach
the right destination, but more like being erased

by an elementary schoolteacher almost ready
to retire. In the rise and fall of her felt eraser, not only
the alphabet but what's left of late spring light
disintegrates into chalk-clouds of quiet indoor winter.
Behind her, the desks, scarred with swear words, hearts

and daggers, are so small that even in imagination
it seems impossible that any child could fit there,
painting a fat gold pancake of sun, a dog floating
over stars, the lopsided mountain of her brown house.
But there she is, at the tiny table, drawing, just as I am,

on a scrap of napkin, a long, soft skein of Z's,
not just sleep's eccentric banner but the alphabet's last
offering, a letter whose first stroke moves forward
as irrevocably as the clock, reverses, then sets off again
to where things start all over, Apple fattening into orchards,

B's green field where someone's always running hard
to steal home, and so on, the soft hinge of daydream
swaying back and forth until it's time to go;
my café table glittering with galaxy swirls
of spilled sugar, the small bill paid hours ago.

THE DEEPEST PART OF THE RIVER

The Goldfish

It was a feeder which means it was supposed
to get fed to something bigger like a barracuda.
But I put the ten-cent comet in clean water
with enough food, no predators and it grew
into a radiant glider full of happy appetite.

That was the truth of it for a long time and then
the fish, for no reason that I could see, suddenly
curled upside down into a red question mark.
Now, its golden scales drop off like sequins
from a museum dress and its mouth forms over

and over the same empty O. Though I wish to
there's no way to free it, not even for a second,
from its own slow death. You say this fish is the least
of it, that I'd better start worrying about what's
really wrong: a child chained somewhere

in a basement, starving; the droop-eyed man,
cooking up, in a cast-iron kettle, germ stew
that will end the world. But that's exactly what I said.
The golden thing is dying right on the other side
of the glass; I can see it and there's nothing I can do.

Fountain Pen Ink, Bottled

I am called *Tinte, Tinta, Encre.*
I am called Ink. Night is my mother.
Her name is *Noir Jais.* Night
is my father. His name is *Tiefschwarz.*
Sometimes I dream of rising out
of my glass house into a tornado's
gutter glossolalia. Sometimes I dream
I have become words so perfect
I am allowed to nest for infinity
in God's butterfly-shaped ear.
Either way, waking remains the same.
Birds who have no relatives in the sky
sip me quickly into wingless bodies
and then for a little while they are able
to fly. At least that is the way it seems.
Those who still remember me: the one
who lives in the egg's gold room
that has no key, a prisoner awake
on death row, all ravens, some crows.

I Want to Be a Ferris Wheel

For Russ Hall

This soft body turned into shining steel,
stretching toward farms and spiders
and the clean windows of the Midwest.
Neon lights on me, that weird kind of green
that a tree wouldn't really recognize
but aliens might, if they happened to be
looking in this direction. A skinny kid,
blond, named Joey, not one tattoo on him,
hits the switch and the big green wheel

just rolls real slow through the darkening air,
like dreaming. Whoever needs to
can sit back and be carried into heaven
over and over. I don't care if there are owls
or stars or clouds or even an Elvis sighting
in the sky, I just want to be carried, everyone
spinning together in this one big circle
that is the same and in the stationary turning
isn't the same at all; air smelling

of ponies and gear grease, burning leaves,
fried dough, the end of summer; everybody
wanting to kiss someone else even if
they're in a seat alone. And my heart,
as dependable as the engine, being fed
by power from some waterfall
full of fat salmon all the guys with hooks
can't figure out how to find; a waterfall
so fierce meteor showers of August

hurl half their fiery selves there to cool off
and not even one scrap of water sizzles.
And the wheel scratching out declarations
of love to wheat fields and empty cinemas,
to garage mechanics in blue coveralls
who still adore every old car with fins
and just this once making a song as stringy
as Christmas lights on plastic palms
in Nevada; a song for cows

still awake in the slaughterhouse,
for the undertaker painting violets
on the dead girl's closed eyes,
for insomniac sisters playing mahjong
by aquarium light; a song for whoever
needs it. In late wind, green wheel
communing with car chrome,
running dreams of collarless dogs
and the electro-deluxe, gone-to-dawn stars.

Dog Harmonica

He's playing the blues for his dog
who would rather be asleep but barks
once in awhile to show he's part of it all
while the guy harmonicas up

a magnolia-shaded road, unpaved, light rain
at dusk, a blue café empty except
for the beautiful waitress, Halley, putting on
Woolworth's cost-a-dollar sunrise-red lipstick,

squinching her lips, kissing the air
where her future's trying to kiss right back,
hard as star-glitter. The kiss is in the music
and it's still raining and now the guy and his dog

are in a blue boxcar, half dreaming the scenery
blurring by—three-legged cat disappearing
into tall corn after the invisible rat;
turquoise river beside a half-burned down church

with its sermon of smoke, dragonflies
skimming the shining water; woman
in a white nightgown walking along
in broad daylight beside the railroad tracks,

real slow, reverizing in a low under-breath song
on Chicky Spark, her in-the-blood love, gone again
on the Midnight Red Eye—his nitroglycerin kisses,
his black boot heel full of diamonds,

his blue ladder almost tall enough to touch
the moon. Her unbound red hair drags in the dirt
behind her, earth studded with mica, shining
like tiny bits of fine, hard honey.

The Nest

I do not have words for the time
I looked at the sky and saw the sunset
making a road and I was walking
down that road but it was not any place
in this world I was walking away from
or to and there were animals in the shadows
but there were no words for the shadows
although I can tell you they were made
of light and the animals were
the animals of God and there was no way
to die on this road that was disappearing
into darkness, into the star-softened horizon
and everything was just as it should have been,
bright and dark at the same time and my name
was beautiful like the nest for the last
singing bird just then beginning
to fall asleep.

A Thing or Two That Might Be True

I was born last daughter
half girl half raven to a candle
maker who was my father
& an arsonist who was my
mother. So many kinds of light
& me with black wings
I had to keep bandaged to my back.
They called me the hunchbacked girl
those who saw me at all.
There were seventeen of us
dwarfs & elephant-eared girls
jugglers & clock-faced boys
babies who looked much like circus dogs
& bayed at the salty far stars.
Oh how I was eclipsed
by every unnatural wonder
a tattered crow girl
with such ordinary feathers.
I grew fueled by the old story
wind told to grass every
night & no one heard but me.
How I longed for air
to carry me to my true country
sky-bride. But for the sake
of my human family I breathed
slow spoke little & dragged behind me
like an old black coat
my sacred & forbidden wings.

Night Sky: window

The fire of dreaming sleeps for a while
in the black grate's ash cradle.
The coffee cup steams. And the egg yolk
from its blue plate, sings about how
the sun loves to bless a late sleeper.
Some of the woman is here. Some of her,
still lying half-awake in the river that runs
through her bedroom, right through one wall
and out the other, water come a long way down
from its home in the mountains, water
as simple as Quaker prayer, flecked
with moss-stars, candelabras of fern.
She drifts on the bed that lifts and floats
as if it were a boat. Sheets waver underwater
like the clean handkerchiefs of surrender.

One Time He Wanted to Be a Bird

This happened near the end of a long winter.
His bird-wanting got stronger and stronger
like a pond getting big water from somewhere else.
The way you come back from sleep
with real kisses still warm on your forehead
from someone you love thousands of miles away.

One day he wakes with red wings, no words
and an infinite love of wind. His wife is not
surprised. She opens the window. She sends after him
a hyacinth-scented kiss. Over snow-capped
backyard barbecues and stalled autos, cold dogs
and sealed-shut cemeteries he flies.

Old woman guarding her husband who wanders
through coma alone; telephone repairman
with handfuls of broken wires in his cold hand,
these are only a few of the ones who see him flying—
wild, wind-tossed rose in dead weather.
And feel a small part of the lost heart return.

Enough, just enough. Does he know this happens?
He knows open sky. He knows being weightless
in the wind. Later, it's not that he stops wanting
to be a bird. He could have lived forever in that red body.
But he misses his wife, woman with a soul full of
Portuguese sunlight, window-opener, kisses

like red hibiscus. So he goes back to being a man.
And that, he thinks, is just as good as flying,
though not the same. But look carefully and
sometimes you will see how he carries inside himself
the mad happiness of trees shaken by spring storms,
the pollen-maps of rapturous bees.

I Don't Know How

I don't know how I'd tell her. I don't think
she'd even want to hear. He's been dead,
now, for years and before that, there was
the divorce and before that thirty years
of booze and heart attacks and beatings.
These days, she flies a lot, visiting the kids,
grandkids but mostly her boyfriend.
So it seems unlikely she'd be happy
to know her ex is waiting there, in Arrivals.

I saw him this last time she came to visit.
He'd gotten through the metal detector
and was sitting with the ticketed passengers
quietly at her gate. It was so clearly my father
that I forgot, for a minute, he was dead.
He was wearing what he always wore, green
work shirt and pants from Sears. His mouth,
open, so you'd look at him and think *baby bird
waiting to be fed*, or maybe *trying to sing*. . . .

"I just make sure she's all right," he said, "and
then I let her go." Though the dead don't talk,
really. It's more like fireflies in early dusk.
You just know what it means and before you can
blink, summer rekindles in your dreaming
from one small spark. He tells me he knows
she'll be staying with the boyfriend in the next
life, too, and *that's all right. That's fine.* He'll
meet her at that gate, too, with roses.

Not like the wild ones that grew on the drunk's
tin shack next door, but store-bought, the kind
he couldn't afford then, this time fancy and safe
in cellophane. He'll help her across and let her go.
Next thing I know some lady's chasing her terrier
right through the metal detector, setting off
an alarm. And then I see my mother making
her slow way out of the shadowy tunnel toward
me, walking right past my father's empty chair.

The Foxy Romaine Produce Box

for Romaine Rebecca Smith Russell & Lysa James

1.
She's only nine or ten, a farm girl,
the century hasn't even turned yet.
She's learned some Latin and so names him
Bonus, good dog, *good.* What she remembers
is the slow search and savor of wild strawberries,
Bonus getting half the haul. Sings to herself.
Braids and braids her auburn hair.

2.
Later, in a steel town so full of factories
most days are night-dark all day long,
she marries, has daughters. Sings in a church
but more often than not, listens to students
slipping off the splintered ladders
of poorly practiced scales.

3.
Her father, war-mean, under the wilted
elm on that Ohio farmhouse lawn,
told her, *Be gracious no matter what.*
Then went right ahead and did
the *no matter what.* Who dares to admit
the beauty of a life they were too afraid
to live? She sang, but not the songs
she meant to sing.

4.
My grandmother's name, Romaine,
means *eternal city* though now, mostly
associated with lettuce. And her last name,
Russell, from Old English,
russel, red fox.

5.
The kind of summer only sleep can invent:
hand-tinted, a hundred years old.
She's been waiting a long time and asks me
please not to forget her. A small girl
in a white sailor dress uses part of a branch
to push a spidery black hoop
to the vanishing point and back.

6.
Years after her death, I'm driving home
but the road is floating, the kind of drift
that insists there's nothing under my tires.
Nothing else, either. No mailman, no dogs,
no moon though the replicas left behind
look real enough. It's trash day
and junk lines every street.

7.
Then, outside a restaurant, there it is,
a huge produce box, blazing red fox
for logo over the lettering FOXY ROMAINE
which doesn't mean a thing to me at first.
But blocks later I realize it's my grandmother,
getting a message through to the living world,
using what's at her disposal. I do a fast U turn.

8.
The trash men arrive just as I do but I want
that box with its sassy red trickster, laughing
as it floats over a huge lettuce that looks
something like our planet but entirely green
instead of lost-in-abyss-blue. Isn't a trap
or piece of poisoned meat can keep this fox
from feeding on stars and getting home safe.

9.
Her message to me is clear.
There's room in this for everything
I love. Trouble is, right now, it's full
of other people's trash. So I jump
right in, lobbing rotten greens out of
the FOXY ROMAINE produce box.
Some tattooed guy, paid to do this,
can't figure why I'm slinging
scummy vegetables, a crazy smile
all over my face like its the Yukon
and I've hit gold. "I want the fox box!"
I sing out. "Take it lady," the guy says,
wide-eyed, "Take anything you want."

The Truth About Why I Love Potatoes

for Sarah Apt

1.
Of everything you get for dinner
they're the most fun to play with:
gravy lakes soaking deep into the soft white Alps
of the mashed ones; French fries good for fences
to keep your fork safe from lima beans;
the baked ones perfect for pounding down
into pancakes from the moon.

2.
I guess I forgot to mention how much I used to love
globbing mashed potato into a ball then hurling it
at my brother so it seemed he was the one
who had made the mess. Now I know grownups
do the same thing, too, but usually not with potatoes.

3.
If a potato were able to turn into a person,
I'm almost certain it would be someone you'd like
for a friend. It could teach you to understand
the language of animals who live underground:
worms and woodchucks, foxes and bears.
On rainy Saturday afternoons, it would take you
to funny movies. When you were feeling sad,
it would remind you of all the good things
you'd forgotten about yourself.

4.
There might be dozens, even more, in the garden,
without you ever knowing, fat moons blooming
a secret night sky right under your feet.

5.
If I could have my wish, I'd want my poem
to be just like a potato. Not afraid of the dark.
Simple and surprising at the same time.
You'd have to dig a little to get it but then
you'd be glad you made the effort. And maybe
after you were finished, something in you
that had been hungry for a long time
wouldn't feel so empty anymore.

If That Boaty Pink Cadillac From 1959 With the Huge Fins

the one that takes up almost two lanes as it swims by,
if it were mine, I'd let you ride in it. I'd pick you up right now,
at your front door. I'd just sit there for a while, hoping you'd look
out the window for a weather test, whatever, and see me
in that huge pink that exists-nowhere-in-nature-czar of a car.

And you'd fly out the door as if a holiday were happening
right in your driveway, as if that millionaire from the old
TV show had finally found your house after all these years,
as if God had said, OK, for the next day despair's
going to have to hold somebody else's soul hostage.

You'd open the Cadillac door, pearly as the nail polish
of Miss Lana Turner, who is now deceased but
whose glamour will never leave us. And wherever you
wanted to go, well, I'd take you there because there's enough
gas in this beauty to get us to Texas or San Francisco

or a good viewing of the shuttle going starward which is what
this bygone baby is, a dream machine with real wheels,
white walls spiffier than anybody's poetry moon,
prettier than Mazda or Toyota, even Infiniti.
A chrome castle soaked in salmony sunrise, a huge pink

thumbs-down to the rat-box subcompact of modern life.
This 1959 Cadillac floating steamy and unstoppable
down the road like a comet the color of Jane Mansfield's lipstick,
melting around corners leaving behind violet flags of old exhaust.
Did I see that? a pedestrian says out loud, What was that. . . .

Well, I'll tell you, that was love's submarine taking its time,
sashaying through the black lack of imagination
all around us. That was me wanting to get you wherever
you want to go and you going right along with it,
in the pink-as-flamingoes chrome cool boat-us-home Cadillac. . . .

Zero Gravity

for Ralph

The storm gets in my phone
and when I lift the receiver I can hear
a polar bear scratching the sky open
to make more snow. But then
the repairman arrives in a red shirt
and climbs the pole and it looks
just like the right-sized rose
has bloomed on the wooden stem.

He gets all the bad weather out
and it doesn't take him long either.
Comes into my kitchen, very quietly,
to computer-check the line.
Just what you'd expect from someone
who goes to the place where the words
have stopped and installs there a river
that can disobey the strongest dam.

Even indoors, the repairman
swims in wind, in all of this,
a bright bouquet of wires in his hand.
You'd have to hold a lot of silence
in you to do this job right.
As he's finishing up, he asks
about the aquarium near the phone
then says, softly, "*I like them so much,*

the fish, that in summer I go out
to the deepest part of the river—that's where
they are—and I am simply with them.
You don't see many. But you know they're there
and that's what matters. I call it zero gravity . . ."
Then he looks up remembering he's not
alone, surprised to have given away
the secret of deep summer solace

in the course of a regular repair.
But it's one and the same thing:
fish touched by all parts of their world
at once, a belonging—an endless, wordless

singing. The repairman moving on
to the next broken thing but not without
leaving my phone full of roses and catfish,
trout and clouds. And I figure if it were

to happen this is the way an angel
would appear—in work boots, in a truck
heavy with the ordinary tools of the world,
hard hat and sky-friendly ladder. A man
who understands the holy language of the fish,
those beings who neither hold nor let go
but simply allow the light current
of the living water to carry them.

WIND OF THE WHITE DRESSES

Physics

The interior of my body's
all galaxy. If you could
open me you'd find
a hut lost in deep forest
glowing with candle-bouquets

the beggar the hermit the witch
left in the lonely room—stars
I saved from the long trip here.
Home through the red meteor shower
of early July.

Such a fine skein of music and skin
seals from sight all this dazzle.
Do you suspect I am making this up?
Why do you think I have never let
anyone see me sleep? I will let you.

Breathe stars with me as I sink into
a boat of light so deep and sweet
and wide that even the most innocent
witness finds the entire blue weight
of earth forcibly an interior treasure.

My soul's such a glitter even sunflowers
in fields hundreds of light years away
lean and dance in my direction.
You say *a conceit, a fantasy.*
I say *physics.* I say *solar wind,*

the secret sheen of my clean blood
and bequeath to you my life.
In passing, I will not spill skyward
with my blue suitcase
of meteors but sink inward

like sequins falling from an opera gown
into a city fountain, like the tiny island
of light a lost coin makes as it's tumbled
into deep ocean. Evidence
of me will remain

though perhaps undetected. My story
is your story. Your story is a tear
that breaks free, shooting star,
sequoia; all night, planets scattering
through random branches.

North, Late April

Public radio. The announcer,
Mozart-rinsed, means to say,
*In the North, flurries expected
to fall* but says, instead, *flowers.*
Before he can correct himself, look—
there they are! roots down, petals
pluming out in parachutes
on a rescue mission: irises
that recall the twilight violet
of Cleopatra's eye, the same
blue of her deep Nile,
then freesias, tulips, daffodils
and a red cancan of azalea.
This cold and leafless place
petal-assailed, saved
by the mistakes desire makes.

The Miraculous Shrine of the Stairway Dime

Fourteen wooden steps to my front door.
On the fifth step, a dime that's lasted there
for years despite dust and brooms, boots that ferry in
mud-lumps and lakes of melting snow.

Finally, to celebrate, I tape next to it
an antique postcard: St. Anne de Beaupre, a blue-
robed, hand-tinted virgin—she has to be a virgin
in a dress that blue, holding aloft

a little man in pink pajamas and this, of course,
is Jesus, gold spikes of light flying from him
straight and strict as a grade school teacher's
admonishments, or a father's: *Sit still.*

Stop singing. Now we will begin our sums.
But I climb past, thinking of my friend in seminary
how the dime would not be enough
to reach him now, how letting go means just that.

And where I see the miraculous star
of God's heart holding steady, I am afraid
he would describe a riot of blasphemy. But I know
this: as a child, he'd put his pillow

on the windowsill waiting
for the visitation of satellites
and shooting stars. How later, his mother
would smooth his dew-drenched hair then draw him

back gently without waking him
into the dark and starless room,
a child still shining
from the far worlds he had been touched by.

It is Ordinary, I Am

awake though well on the way
through the secret door into sleep.
The one painted the same color
every night. But this time
I can see the start
of the world. That far back.
No *I*, just light, indigo
as a dragonfly's wing,
the blue of day but farther
back than that. No air,
no earth, no sun. Simply
the beginning. We are making
the world and there is only
one of us
though soon we will separate
into bodies just
for the joy of it:
anthracite, protozoa, tree frog,
human being. I am awake
in incorporeal levity as *we*
or *I* or that one in indigo
vertigo invents air to remind
my lungs of the blue treasure
they fill with, then spill
to you, who holds the gift
for a heartbeat before
passing it
into thrush's warble.
A miraculous alchemy
calculated into all of memory
shared equally—by breathing—
among priests half asleep
in the dark
confessional, husks
of deep-sea dreaming abalone,
the truth of it shining
even in a forest pebble. I was
awake but I did sleep later
because I could see how simple
it all was and I knew
I would remember.

To the One Lost on the Other Side

When you drown I pull you from the lake
and breathe into you a knowing
until you rise, flame, into the sun's
luxury of resurrection,
until you spill home again, unlikely, alive,
orphan of the hourglass.
I scratch your story into a bar of soap
then wash my hands, as Irina taught me.
So I will remember.
So it is not written.
So there is no evidence to be used
against. I will step in front
of the bullet for you or the knife, stand
whole as the bone noose of a hand
closes at my throat. I have done this.
I will do this. I will be
a sundial bleached white
while the prophets preach heat, preach
flare, teach the blue
chastity of flash fire. Your life
lived in secret, a hut of ice built
on even thinner ice and the thaw coming.
Come home with me. I will feed you. Here is clean
water, the wishbone. Here are some black plums.

Note: Irina Ratushinskaya was held in solitary confinement by the Soviets and
forbidden to write. She scratched her poems with matchsticks on bars of soap,
memorized them and then washed her hands.

All Hallow's Eve

A mouse gnaws a hole
in the white grain sack of sky.
Night spills everywhere.

Small ghost racing
for a hiding place but only fields
loom up wide and starless and low.

Knotted tight at wrist and neck—
the dirty bedsheet she will have
to live in for as long as red leaves fall.

And what costume is he wearing
this time—Raphael, Lucifer,
father? Tall as the balding moon,

he splits a doll's face as he steps
near enough for the flames
stitched into his sour wings

to scissor their golden tips
deep into his daughter's
lamé skin.

The Clearing

Behind the house, a few
hag-scrappy forsythias.
The place raked leaves
were dumped and left
to rot. Also, a ring of trees,
enough for me to call
the woods and go there
every chance I could

where an ancient man
once in a while would step
out of the center
of a maple and help
his equally ageless wife
through a doorless trunk
into the small dark clearing.

They never spoke, never
fought. It was enough,
in a world where there was
no place safe but here,
that they wanted to be
with me. He was thin
as wind. She always wore

a hood the same color
as sky. If it was dark,
small lights speckled the cloth.
If it was storm, he could fly.
They loved me larger
than night and knew,
of course, the terror
our red house held.

It hurt them terribly to leave
the center of the tree—
as hard for them to find
this world as it would be
for a child to try and push
a paper doll through an iceberg

but they were,
my memory tells me,
there, never one without
the other, more whole
than flesh and blood,
secular and
simple as the rain.

Death

When I got there it was
very quiet. Late afternoon.
The porch, empty.
Everyone had gone home.
I slept for a while
in my mother's deep song
of exhaustible sun then woke
just before the first cool air
blew out the green lamps
of the enormous summer trees.

Good, I Said

Got them home—lace-up, black,
high-heeled. Walked in them
and knew what I had done.
Couldn't take a step
without holding my breath
they hurt so much.

Good, I said, I deserve this
for loving a married man,
for paying,
in the first place,
two hundred dollars
for a pair of shoes.

I wore them until I had
no memory of how
it even started.
To look at me
you would not have known
a thing was wrong.

I moved with grace.
I said, until it was inbred,
"Surely, in time,
this will become bearable,"
breath held
in a hobble. Seven years.

Until today.
February 1989, the 23rd.
Ground frozen. Snow predicted.
The litany that kept them
laced: *You paid for this.*
You paid.

No matter how big
the mistake, you have to keep
what you bring home.
But this time, I heard.
Right there on the street,
right then

I unlaced them
and took them off, placed them
side by side
and walked away.
I looked back once
and there they were,

stricken, shrunken.
Me, I turned toward home
my feet cold but comfortable
in three-dollar
cotton socks,
the color, azure.

Strauss and the Cows of Ireland

From my room at dusk I watch
the cows in their late graze.
Great clouds of gnats hang over
them, gauzy as a bride's bouquet.
Downstairs, a radio.
Soprano's aria swells
so delicate and pure
it must be unrequited love
but just what the opera is
I can't tell from here,
though later learn: Strauss,
Der Rosenkavalier.
Cows continue to drift
the dusky pasture, luminous,
as if fed on candlelight
instead of grass. They pass
with heavy gentleness, now
and then stopping to lean toward
our windows with little regard
for human arias that reach them
though it conducts
through me a sweetness:
distant opera and the wandering
of star-tiaraed cows in darkness.

A Little Bit of Timely Advice

Time you put on blue
shoes, high-heeled, sequined,
took yourself out dancing.

You been spending too much
time crying salty
dead-fish lakes into soupspoons,

holding look-alike contests
with doom. Baby, you
need to be moving. Ruin

ruins itself, no use unplanting
what's left of your garden.
Crank up the old radio

into lion-looking-for-food
music; or harmonica, all indigo,
breathing up sunrise. Down

and out's just another opinion
on up and over. You say
you got no makings

for a song? Sing anyway.
Best music's the stuff comes
rising out of nothing.

Dreaming Space Awake

For a while, the mailman stashes Zane Grey and Louis L'Amour
in his mail sack and in each short stretch
between apartments, squirrels and winter-weary shrubs—
he reads a fenceless, stateless, still-forested America back

into place. Between your house and mine,
whole Montana prairies dappled with wild horses.
Halfway to the marine-green mail holding box,
a Lakota Sioux behind a pine, shy

as the wing-singing of returning swans you half-hear
through thick, housed-in sleep. The Government
slow to catch on, finally informs the mailman it's illegal to read
on the job. So he goes farther back

than wild west to first west and now he carries
in his raw, rough satchel, the mail, of course,
but also dozens of tiny plastic dinosaurs he gives to kids
and sometimes me. Just yesterday, a grey stegosaurus

delivered with the electric bill. There's more
than overdue notices being delivered here, more
than catalogues or grocery deals. Between my house
and yours, huge blue beasts from the beginning

link up the entire neighborhood just as easily
as electrical wires and their transformers
or the 3 A. M. dreams that make roads we all meet on,
dance down and waking, erase

while the mailman, day after day, keeps walking,
a weather-blessed tumbleweed seeding in among us
the living corsage of the explorer's campfire,
native peoples shape-shifting

into stone and tree, the pterodactyl's leathery wings
a lot more like a mail sack than you might think,
the almost imperceptible breeze alive with the deep slow heave
of the earliest animals, their fern-drenched dreams.

In This Moment

Geranium, broken by the house painter's boot,
still forces open one white blossom.
And the stranger in a blue Chrysler,
prism hanging from his rearview mirror
stops me while I'm dog-walking.
Front teeth missing, he says, "Come closer.
I won't bite. I'd just like to take you out to dinner."

I lie on the hot summer lawn thinking about this
eat or be eaten world; blossoms too fragile
to do more than falter. That's when two women,
eager as talent scouts or animal trainers, approach.
"May we speak with you concerning God?"
And suddenly, I'm flanked, a sentence fragment
in their big parenthesis, lily of the valley-scented.

One's quiet, moral support; the other's a high-pitched
aviary of dark answers. "You do believe in God.
And hope to get to heaven. But just what
do you think God thinks of you? That you are,
by your mortal nature, lazy, selfish, untrustworthy,
weak. And do you know what punishment you deserve
for all your sins?" I could but do not say

*Sin's simply an old archery term that means 'to miss
the mark' and the ground, ladies, is littered with
your well-meant but dull arrows.* Great sheets of sun
sweep the newly mown lawn and one bird
with a red breast beseeches us to try any kind of song
as it flies from its high invisible branch just this once.
I love these ladies in their flower-print dresses,

their Bibles bathed in the enormous darkness
of their pocketbooks, trying to save me, from what? I don't
know. Maybe the toothless man in his blue car full
of rainbows, the severed branch that still blooms or
the branch that breaks and stays broken, all of us
unsaved, partial and as lovely in this
moment as we will ever be.

RED LETTER DAYS

Red Letters

Hot-spit-and-damn of unchartable cargo flashes past,
lightning blessed. Bridge shakes, almost shatters
with the passing. Gone, and then it's gone. Train

rumbling and plummeting out of summer air. Honest
in its passage, shakes bones, blooms hair. Seduces
and then stands you up, hopeless in one long whistle blast,

almost gets you there, getting and getting. Lackawanna
cars swollen with omniscient thunder, coffins, cheap
wine from Hungary. Gives you soot-stained wind,

a lust for the long worthless wheat fields of America.
Makes sealed baggage cars sing out their locked contents:
gladiola, apple, Aunt So-and-So's black lace-up shoes,

a last letter from death row, nothing but snow
sealed under the silk skins of Maine potatoes. Shamelessly
invades the bedrooms of the unhappily married, inventing

their semi-tropical dreams of parole. Prudence, absent
even in the once-was-blue caboose. Won't be back
with its bereaved sheep grazing in the tiny meadow

of a boxcar next to the red letters of separated lovers.
Keeps no schedule, keeps nothing, and keeps going,
mad sweetheart to each steadfast tree it passes,

spits its way into the future, dragging with it
tracks and vantage point, sunset and perspective,
marries them all in a black daze of closed horizon

leaving only a slight sigh in the shaken trees, no birth
of storm, just ordinary dusk, and the common burden
of having to admit that being witness was enough.

The Earliest Maps

In the earliest maps, the ocean advances
in carefully inked-in margins: *As far
as we have gone.* Then, *What we could see
from there.* It's here the world ends
abruptly in a roar of celestial water
that pours far past imagination.

But look at the part marked *Where
we are*, inhabited fat as an anthill.
The mapmaker has drawn in women and men
bending to garden and anvil scarcely
aware there is an edge to anything.
And tangled in their hair so haphazardly

you might not notice, seaserpents bloom
while fish with stubby wings half-glide,
half-flail in the brain's blue
mutiny, a teacup of it but enough
to support even the whale, robed
in brocades of barnacle, shipwreck and star.

Now scan to the map's real ocean far past
Where we have been. There, ungainly beasts
entice the eye as they breed and feast, huge
in size but strange in thought for that
has been painted in, the windows
of their cranial huts thrown open. Look—

bright tapestries of benevolent dreaming—
tiny women push wheelbarrows full
of turnips; a turf-cutter's hearth glows
gold as a grain of sand. And all of earth's
rivers, no more than blue currants, crushed
sweet in the beast's outstretched hand.

Available Light

I'll tell you who
I write for—the houseplants—
outside all summer;
now, first frost, cloistered
in calm, indoor weather, especially
the geranium.

As leggy as any chorus line dancer
it kicks up and up
for whatever difference
one inch makes
in its proximity
to sun.

All that stretching and then
half its leaves
grow gold, drop, as I stoke
the wood stove, layer
myself in sweaters the color
of fire.
I've been told
repeatedly

by nursery people
geraniums won't keep over winter
unless you hang them
upside down in newspaper hoods
in a dark cellar.
As a child,

for punishment, I was made
to stand for hours
in a black stairwell corner
to consider my ill temper
but I knew those walls
were honeycombed
with treasure—

bracelets of Egyptian gold,
red-handled jump ropes, turtles
who could swallow whole lakes

and I used my time
standing in the dark
figuring ways to rescue

what was rightfully
mine. October, I place
the geranium
in the brightest window
I can find
where it shapes itself
to available light
and stays alive.

Growing Stones in New Hampshire

That first year we turned the soil,
charted a garden that even Babylon
might have blessed. But we had not guessed
about the stones,
what a heavy work they would make
for us—something neither of us had foreseen.

Making way for one radish might mean
shoveling up stones the size
of sewing baskets; for cabbage,
dislodging rock that weighed more
than our wood stove; and in exchange
for tomatoes, a boulder bigger than a sofa.

But we got the garden in
and even had a harvest
after slugs and woodchuck, cutworm
and drought. "Next year," we said,
"will be better. We'll build a fence.
At least the stones are out."

In May, when we set spade to soil
there they were again but worse,
as if they had, in the middle of winter,
descended, winnowed back through solid earth
to where we'd first disturbed their sleep,
returned with even their most distant relatives.

One shovel broke and then another.
Seedlings we'd begun indoors failed
for no apparent reason. "Never mind,"
you said, "we'll harvest what we have."
Evenings you inspect that odd, half-turned over
plot. "Looks like a good crop,"

you say, "and easy. No wasted water.
No weeding to be done."
And start to think those stones are yours,
a yield, a kind of sign. "Sculpture,"
you insist and talk of trailing them all the way
to Boston or New York.

Inspiration's Favorite Foods

A freshly baked loaf of black bread where it is rumored that the Brothers Grimm still hide their best stories. Strawberries. Day lilies for salad. And lobster, only if served on a bed of watercress and white violets.
In times of stress, the shy solace of a baked potato. But remember this. Inspiration can, if forced, take nourishment from nothing at all.

Where Inspiration Has Learned a Thing or Two

From the trees because they are the true intuitives.
Palm readers of sunlight and storm, calm interpreters
for any kind of wind, doing most of the detective work
on shooting stars and aurora borealis. Their easy come,
easy go romances with migrating birds scarcely bear
recording and not even the quick cinema jump cuts
from summer to snow bother them. Even if there is snow,
temperature in the minus numbers, something continues
to live, invisible, at the core. Looking at the tree, you might
see in the bare branches only the bones of Babayaga's hand
or the possibility of kindling for your wood stove, owl haven,
or a kind of living elegy blessed on the highest branch
by one thin crow. Of course you could be wrong. What
inspiration looks like is never really what it is.

Inspiration's Anatomy

Begins with the wishbone of a chicken hung with thread
to dry in the kitchen. For weeks it develops the invisible
flesh of wish and desire. Sways, little divining rod, over
the woman washing dishes, chopping onions, rinsing
garden earth from her hands. When it is finally dry it will
weigh scarcely more than petals, drifted loose, from peonies
on the kitchen table. Because the woman is alone, she must
name one wish for her right hand, another for the left, then
split the fragile bone to see which of the desires overrides.
It is one of the conditions of inspiration that things must
come apart before they can be put back together.

If I'd Been Born in Tennessee

I'd have long ago married somebody named
Sweet Pea Russell. Sour mash, shoot, I guess.
And my name'd be Rita Louise. I'd find me
a Chinaberry to sit up in with old blind Henry's
monkey and maybe I'd play the banjo
and maybe I'd just talk monkey talk
and wait for Sweet Pea to come looking.

There'd be no trouble telling how God's
got hold of the mockingbird's throat
making it tell its kind of repeat truth
just in a way you can't quite get hold of.
Or how the Lord's slinked his way
up the spine of the sunflower that leans over
eavesdropping on everything.

Reading aloud would be easier, too; vowels,
those old wheels going no place special
spinning their worn-outness on the red cart
those idiot twins drive around in,
their overalls so dusty you ain't never
gonna tell what color they was to begin with.
There's rules. There's always rules.

But then there's what's got to be done. And if
I went out into the honeysuckle-soaked night
with someone I ain't naming. And if we
laid down on Double Wedding Ring quilts
and never slept the whole time and never
made much mind of if we got caught. Well,
I guess that's my own business. I could give up

reading altogether and look for Jesus
in the garden with his gold scissors
cutting June bugs and poke brush, black
snakes outta my way. I could say
Goddamn, just that and be old,
the oldest woman ever was, without getting tired
of discoursing with whatever passes by—

three-legged mongrel, hunter's moon,
or the reverend who wears the eye patch,
although the Lord ain't taken no sight
out of that eye. Holy past all telling, he talks
with no patience for the primrose path
which I do believe I have walked
all my life, sour mash, shoot, I guess.

How Spring Appears This Time
of Year in New England

In walks this lady, seventy, maybe
eighty, wants the new look, something feisty.
Okay, so I roll her thin hair
then settle her under the dryer, old Queen bee,
right out of a Saturday morning
monster movie.

She's a regular percussion section
rattling through movie magazines
like she's expecting some Latin type
named Rudolpho or Raoul to step out
of an illustration, sweep her off to a savannah,
scorch her with a lion-wild kiss.

I wasn't as careful as I should have been.
Her hair makes like lightning
in thin blue zigzags, a real robot do.
She's got this smile would teach
a tornado patience. I try to give her
the messed up works for free but she pays

in full, washed cash, and you can see her
doing it. She'd soap each bill, pin
them all to a doll's laundry line, chirping
away the whole time—crazy old parakeet
so caught up in percolating her own song
seems to have forgot she's caught in the cage

for keeps. She counts out every coin to the last
shining dime, says, *Only three-years-old,*
I'd steal blueberries, stuff myself fat
as a summer tick, just trying to turn some part
of myself blue. Now you've done it. And you
give it to me for a good price, too.

Two Trout Fresh-Caught for Your Supper

Over the wire from America you said
you caught two trout
then threw them back for my return
so they'll live another month
until I put hook to line and cast
for them myself. You'll travel
to Florida. Life
is quiet and otherwise
fine. But how to translate
that? It's easier to have me gone?
Longing's not to be wasted
over the crow-heavy wires? Or what?

So like me to take
the unspoken things for tangible
trouble ahead. So like you to tell,
abbreviated, what you think I want
to hear. Between us, an entire
ocean, a thousand shades
of indifferent blue.
So I took a walk down
the muddy path, mistrusting
love in every way I could, like throwing
money away or saying the wildflowers
were only terrible blade-bright lies.

Just then, when I had closed against
myself a like a nearly blind man's only
good eye, the wild peacock appeared
trailing its tail like the score
for an erotic opera over cow dung
and grass, its turquoise neck—
a perfect reproach against all doubt,
stark, in the cloud-heaped sky.
Then I walked back to find
the cook in the kitchen alone, "Look,"
she said, "in the pan, two trout
fresh-caught from Newbliss for your supper."

You might, might not, shrug
with nonchalance, call this

transatlantic coincidence.
But we'd both know better.
She cooked them the way
you do, in rich butter, little
salt, few herbs to keep
the flavor their own.
The flesh pink and sweet as all
we'd left unspoken—on each one
a gold slice of lemon, clear
as sun through cathedral glass.

River

"The greatest cutting does not sever...."
—Lao Tzu

Boulders long ago romanced by glaciers—
now a silky murmur of silt—inhabit me

peacefully, and only children, those who sleep
lightly, and the scarred understand.

What passes over, part of the cure:
clouds molded by a tranquil hand, heron-rise,

sunset. The depths are spangled
by a wily host: one trout leaps toward

light-proffered feast and just as fast sinks
back into a providence of clear current.

I am educated only in how things stay
whole but do not wholly stay.

Occasionally thunder booms a scrap
of Old Testament, but a sunrise

freely tosses solace, child's bouquet:
forget-me-not, pinks,

wood violet. Leave me, but I remain
with you and give you leave to be.

THE GOING UNDER
OF THE EVENING LAND

Private Notice

Now the tigers
hunker and slink
down your quiet street.

They surprise
the neat, narrow gardens
with a generous

ferocity. They eat roses,
liars, untrue lovers.
Merely to be touched

by the shadow of one
can keep you
sleepless and weeping

with awe. Their eyes,
as hungry as forest fires,
sweep across your clear

window. The glass does not
ripple or shatter but you
who sleep inside shiver

although this is deep summer,
shiver and begin to dream
that you are loved.

Relations

for Charles Simic

1.   About Caution

Let's say that whole row of crows on the telephone line
is related.

Let's say seventy different conversations are swept along
in the wire
under their delicate claws.

They are cautious only of wind and questionable weather.
Of human words
they know nothing. They could care not less.

In no time at all, they will vanish
into a vise-like horizon,
wise with evening's first clouds.

Caution, caution, little one, is a handkerchief
wet with someone else's tears.

2.   What They Were Like on the Wire

One as auspicious as a thunderstorm,
One with a tin lunch bucket under its wing.
One singing for all the world like a Harvard professor.
One with a piece of turquoise in its beak.
One educated in obituaries.
One not the least bit interested in stars.
One convinced.
One with a strand of yellow hair tucked under its wing.
One with a heart no bigger than a pen point.
One veering toward celibacy.
One convicted of being infatuated with out-of-body travel.
One wanting to cross the road.
One wearing a scarlet eye patch.
One with several onyx-colored wives,
and one, only one that cannot be described.

The Green Gazebo

A man and a woman sit in the green gazebo,
the great dream square of park empty
except for a luna moth which looks,
in the distance, as if someone standing
in shadow were waving to them
the pale handkerchief of surrender.
And stars only this once, fleck
the inestimable dark in the way
that a first light snowfall resolves the black
meadows of December. But this is summer.

And they are still sitting in the gazebo.
Grass at the bottom of the wooden stairs
is so wet with dew one might believe
that earlier in the afternoon, a woman
in a yellow dress sat there,
stringing necklaces. And, distracted,
spilled a glittering vial of glass beads
that now catch and magnify
streetlamp light, shining
with the slight patina of displacement.

In the dark gazebo they talk a little and not
softly. Still the cool air carries away
their words and no one hears.
They hold each other, every advantage
of imagination theirs; the loss they face
for now, as far away as the dead stars,
whose intricate light appears to them as beautiful
as tears caught in the eyelashes of the unaware
sleeper. They will have said goodbye
long before morning approaches the empty park.

What can I say of them to keep them
there a little longer? What is there to say?
That they are happy? That they
are where they ought to be? How flat
that sounds and stupid, really,
when looking at the two of them,
speechless and together—the bright grass
sweeping in a midnight wind,
a casual and worldly blessing
around the green gazebo.

Loneliness

At first the pig is as tiny as a walnut
and so intelligent it answers the phone
taking messages in polite soprano.

She lets it move in, fills its bureau
with acorns, peppermint candies.

Its eyelashes are so long she has to comb them
daily. The pig grows quickly, pink moon,
never quite full.

It eats the dictionary, a kitchen chair,
her favorite hairbrush. Even so,

she allows for it to stay, saying—
A simple case of domestic hunger that has its limits.
The pig continues to eat—

quilts, cooking spoons, the wedding dress
that she has not yet worn.

Eats and eats until it has to eat the living room,
the entire place. Picture this: a pig
as big as a five-room apartment, grinning. . . .

a woman wondering what to do next
when a little door in the pig's side swings open.

It is her dining room she sees inside,
the table neatly set for one, a candle and a rose,
glass platter of uncracked acorns, toy telephone.

Mockingbird

The mockingbird's a live encyclopedia
of song. Listen, it can be
the whole world humming to itself:
tinsel consonant of wind
in love with whatever its silken glove
touches, never touches

and then again it's just the normal chatter
of thrush or grackle.
The mockingbird's own song? Difficult
to hear in this aria that includes
news from every absent bird,
but slightly richer. All night

it stays awake, slipping its glad opera
into the delicate bone cage
of the Emperor's or your sleeping
ear. For this, the glass blower wakes
and weeps, knowing how frail his world is
and imperfect.

Summer

A butterfly lights
on the eyelid
of a woman
sleeping
in the sun.
Light passes through
the stained-glass
window
of one wing:
her cheek
as blue as if
berries had been
crushed there.

The Going Under of the Evening Land

But it should be quite a sight, the going under
of the evening land. . . . And I can tell you, my young friend,
it is evening. It is very late.

—Walker Percy
The Moviegoer

In the evening land, a woman
places fresh bread on a polished table.
She turns on lamps, watching light
make golden maps on tabletop and parquet floor.
Here, without her knowing,
an interior continent completes itself.
She listens

to the glittery chatter of silverware released
from drawers that smell of Chinese tea.
Crows begin sleep now, a few stars
hidden in their pockets of black silk.
In the evening land
she considers how darkness leans cleanly
into its bright double—

how neither leaves for very long. Outside,
a child plays hide-and-seek
with the rosebush ghost. Now between
light and dark, the world splits open
but only a little, what is, what could be.
And in this time, there are words
no one needs to speak:
                              I woke last night

thinking the bed to be an ocean liner
in touch with Antarctica, something
breaking up, something going under.
Tier on tier, the glittery necklace
of the ship sinking, or the iceberg
singing but I was safe, I was
safe and I wanted you to know.

The Will to Live

On the green lawn of a city park
a sentence of dark insects completes itself:

Believe! Believe!
Above, two Monarchs matter and flash

in this immense summer air.
Small scraps of wing, good weather, a will

to live, they come
from the tenuous country of now

whatever the heart is asking for. Even if I
weren't here

they'd still congratulate the sky
with a fragile disbelief in sorrow. Graceful

as the hands of the deaf
they form a language in air that I understand

almost not at all. Being human
I might say

they kiss and part and kiss again, but
know they're governed by desire

or law or lack of these
beyond me. They fling themselves

against a sky so big
they do not understand it's there. Clouds

fat and ample, grow
fatter still and if the old June maples

stand weighed and without words
it is not from human grief, or any other.

NO ORDINARY WORLD

The Whale Poem

I am a swimming forest;
each rib in me
a harp
no wind will hurt
into music.

Make your claim, Eve,
make it.
For garden I depend
not on your god,
not on the hand

of lightning, harsh
scripture of the harpoon.
This planet is blue.
I do not ask
to be forgiven.

The Juggler Defines His Art

It matters little to him. He can take stones
in his hand or birds or bits of burning wood
and storm the sky as sure as a meteor shower.

Ask him how and he will sigh, saying,
"Ah, I have married Lady Gravity
and these, these are my children."

Then ask him what it is
he loves so much that he is able to suspend
all belief in the solid world.

And he will say, "The heart is an orange,
a porcelain cup, a closet
that has not been opened in years.

My own heart I am no longer sure of.
Once it was a golden watch.
I gave it to the woman I loved;

each jewel in that watch, a planet.
Each planet, a place where we were safe.
Now I am no longer sure of anything

but time passing on her lost wrist
as I pass hand over hand, far above
your amazed faces, my bright and weightless life."

The Knife-Thrower's Wife

The knife-thrower's wife stands
stranded in danger's glittery geography.
A paper breast is pinned in sequin
to her breast. She would be afraid
if she could see her husband caress
each knife, mouth her name before aiming.

But the spotlight sews her eyes shut.
Slut, he says to himself, *you whore*.
Now she hears them coming, a sound
like bees, a sound of bullets. She
wonders if there is war somewhere.
Applause, a held-breath pause.

He places his blindfold carefully. He aims
as close to her heart as he can. And then
it is over. She steps forward, sees
her silhouette set out by ice pick,
sword, all manner of sharp things. She
joins hands with her husband. They bow.

She sees he loves his knives more than
he loves life: his, hers, it doesn't matter.
This is what makes her take her place
again and again, glad for the knives
that need her, that wait to surround her
like a crowd of adoring suitors.

The Need to Talk

The poem you asked me to write
places me at this plain table, at a time
when my neighbors lie blessed in pairs;
the evidence, Biblical. Their ark,
sleep which eludes me.

Hardest to bear is the light
from my lamp, late now, in December.
I live alone, would like to believe
this light is more than
the loosely woven cloth of insomnia;

would like to believe my life is more
than what surrounds me. My shoes
surround me, paired up like couples
at a private funeral, each with their own
reasons for walking away.

For a moment I hold my ground,
gaze at the box of paper before me
as blank as calendar pages for next year.
Here, the funeral goes unattended;
love's body lies cold, embossed
by the kiss of a literary rose.

Nothing has died that I cannot do without
but even as I write this, I set my head down
on the table, for a moment,
for a moment only, and wish
there were someone here to talk to.

Walter Bridge's Death by Drowning

1958 - 1972

I wonder why I always do things wrong.
Davis and Earl kept on top
of the lake like rubber ducks.
I dived, watched them disappear.
They survived. Their legs
dangled from a bright sky
like bicycle handlebars, far away.

I reached for air, caught only a rough
rope of water and a minute later
I knew something on the bottom
wanted me. Not the way rats
used to hiss, nibbling my sleep
like I was their gingerbread boy,
brown enough and sweet.

I thought again of Earl, our jelly
sandwiches wax-paper wrapped,
my tennis shoes hidden on shore.
I tried to shout. My lungs filled
with water as easily as if it were air.
Afterwards, I drifted to these weeds.
They wrapped me mummy-tight,

murmuring apologies. I never
knew my mother. The weight
of nothing presses me as flat
as fresh ironed sheets. Dusky
streets chalked for hopscotch
tighten at my neck. I' made of lead,
late for school, can't run.

There's something scared inside
wants out, can't shout anymore.
I am the one who did not
get away, thin as the reeds
that surround me. Whoever I was,
Walter Bridges, now rises empty
and aching in the swollen sun.

No Child of Earthly Kitchens

I owned no raincoat and in the season of storms
was sent to school under my mother's umbrella.

It was the color of pale sherry. The ivory handle
kept about it the faint smell of perfumed wrists.

It never carried me away although I wished it
often enough that I can still see beneath me

people with their umbrellas like black morning glories
growing small on a polished street.

And I see, too, my house as tidy as the shoebox
for a hurt bird; the flat horizon

filling out as purple and plump as an eggplant.
And when the dark arc of the umbrella sets me down

and when my feet again touch stubborn ground
I am no longer a child of earthly kitchens

but find the geometry of clouds closeted in my heart
and in my hair, the strange blue perfume of storm.

Part of a Family History

In the room where my grandmother
used to sit, the window
still admits light as if
that light were the arrival of a friend,
arms folded around a cloud
of Queen Anne's lace. Even now
it seems she is there
in a green-print summer dress
waiting for me, the dark stones
on her fingers shining between us
like secrets. But she is
not there and when she left
she took my name for her last word
saying it quietly and I did not come
saying it once again
and the dark door opened.

Meditations Before and During Sleep

Consider the waltz; consider bears
that dance in spite of chains, their fur
scarred by ticks and disobedience.

Consider your loneliness; the mailbox
empty except for a mockingbird's nest,
the mirror that promised you everything
and then went blank.

And think of rooftops at dusk
as if they had been drawn by a child
who is wearing a light-blue smock;

your hands as they sleep
remembering a weight of pearls,
bodies they have memorized,
departures they have signaled.

Consider the anagram of sleep
in which you have just created yourself.

Silence grows like a white camellia
from the mouth of the mime
and the walls with their inner chambers
keep secret the shoes of your childhood.

Consider that somewhere in a room
just beginning to grow dark,
in Montana maybe, or Wyoming,

someone folded among shadows
is saying, softly, your name.
Consider those shadows, the one
red geranium left out on the stairs,

straining and stretching there in the wind
of a passing train, its dry bright leaves
for nearby rain, for news of the distant sea.